Old-Fashioned Ribbon Trimmings and Flowers

Mary Brooks Picken

DOVER PUBLICATIONS, INC.

New York

Ribbon flowers on cover courtesy of C. M. Offray

Bibliographical Note

Old-Fashioned Ribbon Trimmings and Flowers, first published by Dover Publications, Inc. in 1993, is a slightly altered republication of *Ribbon Trimmings and Flowers: Instruction Paper with Examination Questions,* published by Woman's Institute of Domestic Arts & Sciences, Inc., Scranton, Pennsylvania in 1922. The book has been reset in a new format, slight corrections have been made and the examination questions have been omitted. A new Publisher's Note has been written for this edition.

Library of Congress Cataloging-in-Publication Data

Picken, Mary Brooks, 1886–
   [Ribbon trimmings and flowers]
   Old-fashioned ribbon trimmings and flowers / Mary Brooks Picken.
      p.   cm.
   Originally published: Ribbon trimmings and flowers, Scranton, Pa. : Institute of Domestic Arts & Sciences, 1922.
   ISBN 0-486-27521-3 (pbk.)
   1. Ribbon work. 2. Ribbons. I. Title.
TT850.5.P53 1993
746′.0476—dc20
                                                                         93-2506
                                                                            CIP

Manufactured in the United States of America
Dover Publications, Inc., 31 East 2nd Street, Mineola, N.Y. 11501

PUBLISHER'S NOTE

IN THE 1920s, trimming clothing and accessories with ribbon was considered very "smart." Today, not only is it smart, it is lots of fun! There has been a veritable explosion of color and texture in the ribbon industry, and the variety of ribbons available is staggering. Along with old favorites like satin, velvet and grosgrain, you will also find mesh ribbons, organza ribbons, wire-edged ribbons, print ribbons, plaid ribbons and more.

Most of these ribbons are suitable for at least some of the trims shown here, although cut-edge ribbons intended primarily for crafts may not stand up to the repeated handling required for some of the more intricate trims.

This book was originally intended as a textbook for aspiring dressmakers and milliners and contained, in addition to the instructions, examination questions to test the student's mastery of the subject. We have omitted the exam and changed the format, but all the instructions needed to make the trims are here.

In *Fig. 2*, you will find a chart illustrating ribbon widths. As stated in the book, this chart was not used by all manufacturers even at the time. Today, it is even less universal. However, although ribbons are sized by number, on a retail level at least, they are more usually sold by width. We have left the chart as it originally appeared, because it gives a general idea of ribbon sizes and because many of the instructions refer to the numbers. You can easily compare the numbers to the chart to see what width is called for.

Some of the materials mentioned may be unfamiliar to you. In some cases, terminology has changed; in other cases, the item is no longer being manufactured. However, substitutes can easily be found for everything needed to make the trims.

The cabochon foundations mentioned on page 24 are no longer readily available. However, a circle or oval of heavy interfacing, needlepoint canvas (either fabric or plastic) or of cardboard may be substituted. If you need to have a rounded form, you can glue graduated layers of quilt batting to the form, but a flat surface usually works just as well. For example, for the daisy shown on the cover, the petals are glued to a circle of plastic canvas. The French knots are worked directly onto a separate circle of needlepoint canvas which is glued on top of the petals. If you intend to sew the ribbon to the form, add a layer of batting and cover the form with fabric.

Instead of covering the wire stems of the flowers with green rubber tubing as suggested in the instructions, wrap them with self-adhesive florist's tape.

The modern glue gun can simplify the construction of many of the flowers and trims. Instead of tacking and attaching with thread, you can tack and attach with a spot of glue. All of the flowers on the cover were made with a glue gun. As you read over the instructions, you will, no doubt, find other ways to incorporate new methods and materials.

The trims can be used in a myriad of ways. Make a rosette for the lapel of a special suit, spruce up an old straw hat with rosebuds, decorate a wall wreath with a bunch of grapes, add a pleated band around the edge of a decorative box, wrap the classiest gifts in town—the possibilities are limitless. Use this book as a starting point and let your imagination run wild.

TABLE OF CONTENTS

RIBBONS

DESIGNATION OF WIDTHS

A **ribbon** is a band of silk, satin, or velvet, with selvages woven on both edges. Ribbons vary in width from ⅛ in. to 9 in., although during recent years ribbons wider than 9 in. have been made. Among manufacturers, the widths of ribbons are stated in *lignes* (pronounced *lines*). Gauges marked in lignes are made, so that the purchaser of ribbons can measure them and determine just how many lignes there are in each width of ribbon. *Fig. 1* (page 2) shows a gauge, or rule, graduated in lignes along one edge and in inches along the other. The relative sizes of the ligne and the inch can readily be seen in the illustration, which shows the actual sizes. The ligne is a French measure that is used almost exclusively by manufacturers in selling ribbons to wholesale and retail dealers; but retailers sell ribbons by the yard. The manufacturer sells ribbons by the bolt and bases the price on the width in lignes. A *bolt* of ribbon is a roll of ribbon approximately 10 yd. long.

The common way of designating the various widths of ribbons is to use numbers. These numbers range from 1 to 250, the smaller numbers indicating the narrower ribbons and the larger numbers the wider ribbons. *Fig. 2* (page 2) shows a ribbon gauge that indicates the widths of satin ribbon corresponding to the different numbers as adopted by the most reliable manufacturers. Unfortunately, however, some ribbon manufacturers ignore this gauge and use one of their own, in which the various widths are narrower than those corresponding to the several numbers in *Fig. 2*. Thus, a No. 100 ribbon made by one manufacturer may be considerably narrower than a No. 60 made by another manufacturer, whereas it ought to be wider. Because of the difference in standards, then, the purchasing of ribbons by merely stating the number may result in disappointment, as the purchaser may get a ribbon much narrower than she requires. To avoid error and trouble of this kind, it is a good plan to cut a paper gauge to the width of ribbon desired and then to buy the ribbon that corresponds most nearly to this gauge; or, if desired, the width of ribbon required can be stated in inches and fractions of an inch, and the nearest corresponding width of ribbon can then be obtained. For velvet, grosgrain, and other ribbons, the numbers of lignes corresponding to the various widths differ slightly from those given in *Fig. 2*.

USES OF RIBBONS

The use of ribbons for dress ornamentation are so varied that to enumerate them would be a severe task. However, when a gown is finished, difficulty is seldom encountered in deciding how to strengthen or enhance it by means of ribbon ornaments or trimmings of certain colors or combinations of colors. Thus, a rose, a rosette, or a bow at the waist line, a tiny bud at the shoulder, or a little narrow strip of attractively finished ribbon tastefully arranged around the neck will often-times add a smartness to a frock that is difficult to obtain in any other way. Many times a garment that looks very ordinary may be improved wonderfully by an artistic arrangement of ribbon in the form of a bow, a rosette, or a flower. Indeed, such trimming will serve to give tone and strength just where it is needed and add greatly to the general effect or appearance.

Bows for little girls' dresses, for sashes, and for the hair are practically a necessity. For example, there is nothing prettier to behold than a dainty frock neatly made and trimmed with attractive bows of delicate pink, orchid, or blue. Many times a soft yellow or cream is used for such purposes, but seldom are any of the other tints employed.

Lingerie garments, likewise, offer great possibilities for the use of ribbon trimmings. Seldom is an elaborate night dress, corset cover, or petticoat made without ribbon placed somewhere upon it.

The ribbon trimmings, bows, and flowers given in this book are presented with the thought of giving the correct rules for the development of the different kinds. The making of such bows and trimmings is usually very simple when the correct handling of ribbons is understood. Therefore, for the best results, it is advisable to make up all the trimmings taken up in this book, no matter in what form they may be. This plan not only will be the means of making every detail clear, but will be the means of obtaining a supply of trimmings that will be valuable for many purposes.

In connection with the study of this book, it is advisable to note such things in the shops, for when the making of the various trimmings is thoroughly understood it will be possible to duplicate satisfactorily any ribbon bow, flower, or other trimming that may be seen. In this way, many of the attractive things that are brought out from time to time with style changes can be produced with very little effort.

The colors of the ribbons in nearly every case may be either harmonizing or contrasting with the garment with which they are to be worn. In making any kind of trimming, it is advisable to use as good material as possible. If the ornament is to be made of ribbon, therefore, it should be of good quality and of as rich a shade or as delicate a tint as possible, and the same thought applies for silk or velvet pieces that are to be used in the making of such articles.

0 FRENCH LIGNES
6
12
18
24
30
36
42
48
54
60
66
1
2
3
4
5
6

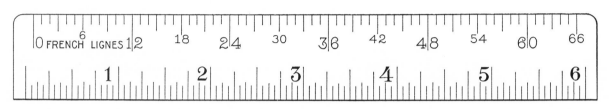

Fig. 1

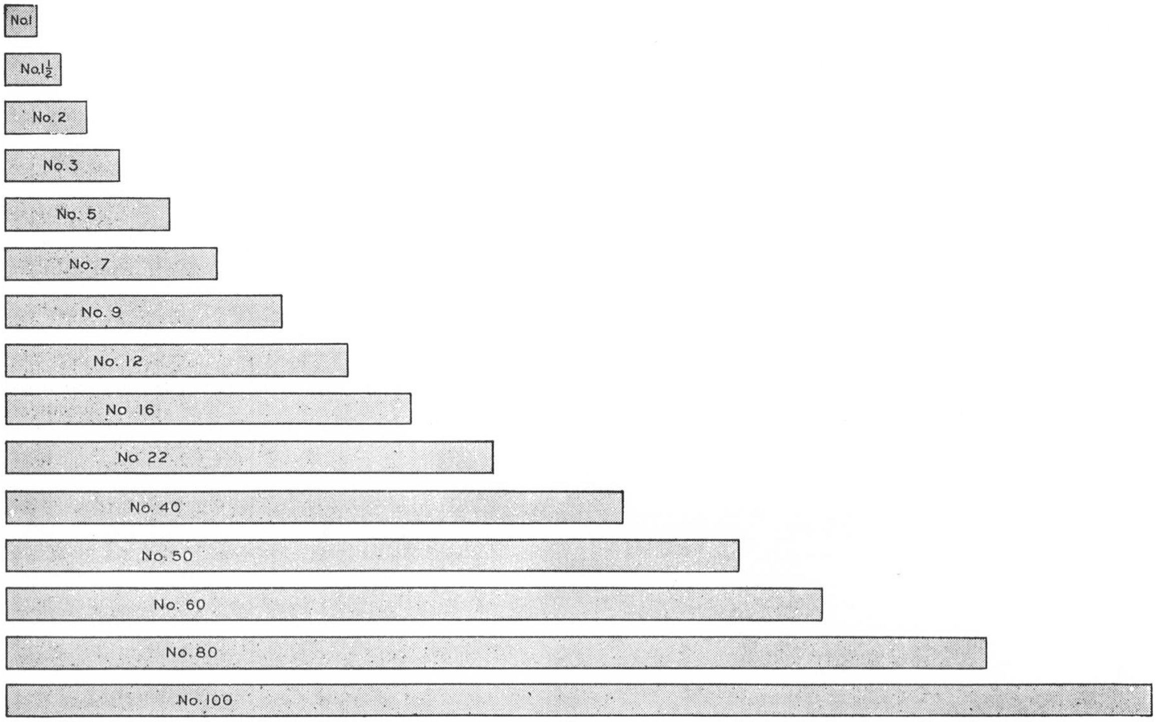

No.1
No.1½
No. 2
No. 3
No. 5
No. 7
No. 9
No. 12
No 16
No 22
No. 40
No. 50
No. 60
No. 80
No. 100

Fig. 2

FLAT RIBBON
TRIMMINGS

RUFFLED AND PLAITED RIBBONS

Among the simplest forms of ribbon trimmings are those made by ruffling, or gathering, and plaiting. Numerous examples of ruffled and plaited ribbons are given in the succeeding illustrations. It will be observed that the thread used in ruffling and in making the plaits differs in color from the ribbon itself. This is done in order that the gathering thread will show clearly in the illustrations. In the actual making of fancy garnitures, however, the thread used should match the color and luster of the ribbon. The various shirred and plaited ribbons shown in the illustrations are used as trimming on skirts, sleeves, collars, and revers, especially on mature women's coats. They are used also on the edges of scarfs and for numerous other purposes.

Ribbon Gathered in the Middle. A ribbon gathered by hand in the middle and used for many of the purposes mentioned is shown in *Fig. 3 (a)*. In order to have the gathering thread exactly in the middle, it is necessary to mark the line to be followed. Therefore, fold the ribbon directly in the middle and press it on the wrong side with a moderately hot iron, or press it between the thumb and the forefinger. Then gather the ribbon along the line of the crease thus made, using very short stitches, as shown at the left in the illustration. The length of ribbon to be used for making a ruffle of this kind must be one and one-half times the length of the space to be covered. For example, if a ruffled ribbon is to be placed on the outer edge of a collar that measures 36 in. around, the length of ribbon required to make a ruffle of the proper fulness will be 1½ × 36 = 54 in., or 1½ yd. In making such ruffles, it is advisable not to break the thread from the spool until the gathering has been finished.

The sewing-machine ruffler may be used for gathering ribbons. A ribbon in which the ruffling is done by machine is shown in *Fig. 3 (b)*. The ribbon should first be creased in the middle, as in making a ruffle by hand, so that the crease may be used as a guide in gathering. A very small, fine stitch should be used for gathering, or ruffling.

Ruffled ribbons like the one shown in *Fig. 3*, whether made by hand or by machine, should be attached to the garment by machine-stitching or by a very short backstitch on the upper side and a long stitch underneath.

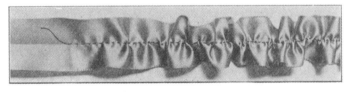

(a)

(b)

Fig. 3

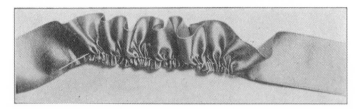

Fig. 4

Fig. 5

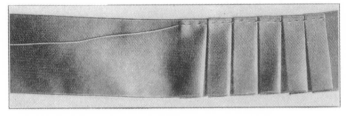

Fig. 6

Ribbon Gathered Along One Edge. Ribbon may be gathered along one edge, instead of in the middle. *Fig. 4* shows a piece of ribbon that has been ruffled along a line close to one of the selvage edges with a machine ruffler. Ruffles of this sort are used where a cluster of ruffles is desired, for borders on scarfs, or for the outer edges of other ruffles where great fulness is desired.

Ribbon Gathered Zigzag. A narrow ribbon gathered by a zigzag running-stitch is illustrated in *Fig. 5*. Ribbon so gathered is commonly known as *shell trimming;* also, it is called *purled ribbon* by milliners. In order that the gathers may be even and similar, guide lines must first be marked, as shown. Lay the ribbon on the ironing board with the right side up. Pick up the right-hand end of the ribbon and draw it down so that the ribbon is folded, and so that the top selvage edge lies squarely across the ribbon, in line with the grain of the silk. Press the fold with an iron, and open it out and the ribbon will then show one bias crease. Pick up the same end of the ribbon again and draw it upwards, so as to make a second bias fold running in the opposite direction to the first crease and meeting the first crease at the edge of the ribbon. Press this fold with the iron, making the second crease. Then open up the ribbon, fold it over toward the bottom, so that the third crease pressed in will be a bias crease parallel to the first crease made and meeting the second crease at the top. Open up the ribbon, turn the strip upwards, make the fourth crease, and continue in this manner until the entire piece of ribbon has been properly creased. Start the gathering near one end and follow the line of creases. Draw the thread tight enough to draw the ribbon together, as

shown, but take care not to have greater fulness at one place than at another.

Single Knife-Plaited Ribbon. A piece of ribbon on which single knife plaiting has been done by hand is shown in *Fig. 6*. The length of ribbon required for this kind of plaiting is three times the length of the part that is to be covered. Thus, if a band of knife-plaited ribbon 24 in. long is needed, the amount of ribbon required to make the band will be $3 \times 24 = 72$ in., or 2 yd. In order to get the plaits of the same width and evenly spaced, gauges should be used. From a strip of thin cardboard or an old postal card cut four gauges, each as wide as the desired plaits and about 2 in. longer than the width of ribbon to be plaited. Take special pains in cutting these strips to have them of equal width throughout. Lay the piece of ribbon wrong side up on the work table, and secure the end to the table by tacking or pinning. About 1 in. from the end farthest from you lay one of the gauges squarely across the ribbon, so that its upper end is ¼ in. below the top edge of the ribbon, and hold it in position with the finger. Bring the ribbon back over the gauge and crease it exactly in line with the edge of the gauge that is closest to you. Lay a second gauge exactly on top of the first. Bring the ribbon over the gauge and crease it at the edge of the gauge that is farthest from you. Then lay another gauge below the first two and on top of the ribbon, the edge of the gauge coming exactly in line with the edge of the first two gauges and not overlapping or separating in any place. Next, bring the ribbon over in the same manner as before and crease it at the edge of the gauge. Then place another gauge and proceed in the same manner. If the plaits do not hold well by creasing with the finger, a moderately hot iron should be at hand so that the plaits may be securely pressed in position. As the plaiting is proceeded with, gently remove the gauges from the plaits that are made and use them for succeeding plaits. In order to keep the plaits absolutely straight, it is advisable to watch the edge of the gauge and keep the end of the ribbon exactly parallel with it. Likewise, as the plaiting is continued, baste the plaits in position on the right end edge, so that there will be no danger of their coming out, especially if there are several yards of plaiting to be made, as it is impossible to keep it flat on the table until all the plaiting is finished.

Double Knife-Plaited Ribbon. A double knife-plaited ribbon is illustrated in *Fig. 7*. Such plaiting is done in much the same manner as the single knife plaiting. Gauges are used to insure perfectly even plaits, but eight are required instead of four. The first plait is made as in single knife plaiting, but instead of making the second plait alongside of the first, it is made directly on top of the first and in the same way as the first. When the second plait is completed, there are four gauges in the plaits, one directly over another. The third plait is then made below the first two, and close to them, after which the fourth is made directly on top of the third. The four plaits are basted or pinned in position, the gauges are removed from the first and second plaits, and the fifth and sixth plaits are then made. The work is continued until the required length of plaiting is done. The length of ribbon needed for making double knife plaiting is five times the length of plaiting desired.

Single Box Plaiting. Box plaiting may be used as a substitute for ruffling, if desired. Single box plaiting, like single knife plaiting, requires three times the amount of material to make a given quantity of plaiting. Half-inch plaits, both in knife plaiting and box plaiting, may be taken as a standard size, because they work up to good advantage for almost all purposes.

The single box plait is made by the use of gauges, the same as in making the single knife plait. The first plait is made by using two gauges, the next plait being made directly on top of the first plait, using two more paper gauges, as when making the double knife plaiting; but instead of being sewed down, the second plait is first turned back toward the left and then sewed in position as in *Fig. 8*. While the illustration shows the row of stitching in the middle, the box plait can be made and sewed down at one edge. The third plait is made to fit up close to the second plait; the fourth plait is made the same as the second and turned back to the left. The work is continued in this manner until all the plaits have been made.

Double Box Plaiting. Double box plaiting is illustrated in *Fig. 9*. Such plaiting is done in exactly the same way as single box plaiting, except that two plaits are first made and folded to the right, and then two more are made on top of these and turned back to the left. The work is continued in this manner until the required number of plaits have been made. The stitches, if drawn tight at the middle of the ribbon, will force the edges of the upper box plait to come almost together at the top, as shown at *a* and *b*. The length of ribbon required is five times the length of the strip of plaiting to be made.

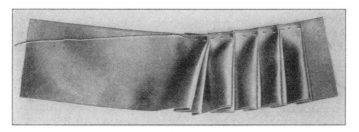

Fig. 7

Fig. 8

Fig. 9

Fig. 10

Triple Box Plaiting. Triple box plaiting is shown in *Fig. 10*. It is made in the same manner as the single or double box plaiting, with the exception that there are three plaits one on top of another with the folds to the right, and three similar plaits with the folds to the left. In either double or triple box plaiting, the centers of the top plaits may be drawn together with stitches as at *a* and *b*, in order that the plaits will fold over and cover the row of stitching in the middle of the plaiting. If, however, this stitching is carefully done by hand, using very short stitches on the right side, the line of stitching will be practically invisible. Triple box plaiting in light-weight narrow ribbon is frequently used for the edges of fichus, scarfs, and baby bonnets. The ribbon used must be seven times as long as the strip of triple box plaiting desired.

RIBBON PETALS AND BEADING

Ribbon Petals. A band of ribbon may be covered with petals made of ribbon, after which it may be made up into various forms and designs. Petals of the same general form, but with slight variations, may be used in making rosettes, as well as fancy trimmings for the edges of collars, cuffs, and vests, skirt bandings, etc. The ribbon petals referred to may be made of any width of ribbon; however, widths Nos. 9, 16, 22, and 40 are the ones most frequently used. The ribbon must be cut into separate pieces, one for each petal, and the length of each piece must be exactly twice the width of the ribbon, as shown in *Fig. 11 (a)*. Lay the piece face downwards on the table and turn in the upper right-hand corner *a* so that the cut edge *a b* of the end of the ribbon will lie even with the selvage edge at the bottom and the corner *a* will be at the middle point of the bottom edge, as in *(b)*. Likewise, turn in the upper left-hand corner *c* of the ribbon so that the cut end *c d* of the ribbon will lie even with the bottom selvage of the strip and the corner *c* will meet the corner *a*. Stick a pin through the corners to hold them in position, and turn the piece over so that the selvage opening *e* is at the back. Fold over the left-hand point of the ribbon until the point is even with the bottom selvage and slightly passes the center of the petal, as in *(c)*, and tack it in position with a stitch or two, as shown, so that it will not slip. Then fold over the right-hand point in exactly the

same manner so that it passes the center of the petal, and tack this point to hold it in place, completing the petal, as shown in *(d)*.

Sewing Petals on a Band. After a sufficient number of petals have been made as just described, they may be sewed on a band, as shown in *Fig. 12*. First cut the band of ribbon of the length required. Baste the first row of petals edge to edge near the top of the band and stitch them fast. Baste and stitch the second row of petals ½ to ¾ in. below the first row, being careful to have these petals cover the bottom of the first row and hide the stitching. Baste the third row on exactly the same distance below the second as the second is below the first, and stitch it down. The band of ribbon must be wide enough so that the bottom edge can be turned back to cover the bottom row of petals, after which the turned-back piece of the band and also the petals are stitched, as shown.

Such bands may be used on straight edges or flat surfaces. If it is desired to make the band in the form of a rosette, a fine wire should be run through the hem of the ribbon at the bottom, as shown, and the band should be pushed together tightly on it, as shown at the left-hand end. The amount of ribbon required for a band of this kind is governed entirely by the width of the ribbon used and the size of the ornament desired.

Beading. The form of ribbon trimming shown in *Fig. 13* is known as *beading*. The parts representing beads are made by the use of small, compact cotton balls or wooden button molds whose diameter is half the width of the ribbon used. Fold the selvage edges of the ribbon over so that they meet at the back, and near the end of the ribbon wrap the thread around tightly, as at *a*. Take a couple of stitches through the ribbon at this point to keep the thread from unwrapping. Through the opening at the back, push inside the fold of ribbon thus formed a cotton ball or a button mold. Draw the ribbon tightly over the ball or mold, wrap the thread around close to it, as at *b*, and fasten the thread with a couple of stitches. Insert another cotton ball or button mold, wrap the thread around the ribbon, as at *c*, and continue in this manner until a sufficient quantity of the beading has been made. Such trimming is very desirable on chiffon and maline dresses and draperies. If it is impossible to secure cotton balls or button molds made of wood, old beads may be substituted.

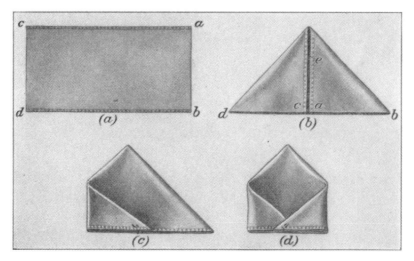

Fig. 11

Fig. 12

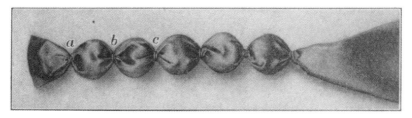

Fig. 13

RIBBON BOWS

The one thing that stamps the true artist is the making of a ribbon bow. One reason for this is that the material in itself, like a pile of rough lumber, may be fashioned into an endless variety of wonderful things. A piece of ribbon might be wrapped around the waist perfectly plain, making a sash and answering the purpose for which it was intended; yet the same piece of material, when manipulated by the deft fingers of a skilful person, can be fantastically fashioned into a bow of wondrous beauty.

A piece of ribbon of good quality, manipulated by one possessing ingenuity and creative and constructive ability, can readily be looped and twisted into forms of bows that will merit the admiration of all who may have an opportunity to see them. There are a number of exceptionally important points to know and remember in purchasing ribbons to be used for certain purposes and places. Soft, light-weight, pliable ribbons are best adapted for making short loops; heavy-bodied ribbons, such as grosgrain and peau de soie, are best adapted for plain bands and flat bows; while the stiffer, heavy-faced satin ribbons should be purchased for the making of ribbon flowers. Messaline ribbon, which is a soft silk ribbon having a shiny surface, should be used for tied loops and short loops.

In the construction of ribbon bows, care should be taken not to handle the ribbon more than is absolutely necessary. Much of the beauty of ribbon bows lies in the freshness of the ribbon, which may be completely destroyed by careless handling. For the same reason, too many stitches should be avoided in making bows with the aid of needle and thread. After a bow has been completed, it must be sewed securely in position; but the stitching should not be so tight as to draw the bow out of shape and cause it to lose its daintiness or be less attractive.

The principal object to be attained in making ribbon bows is to have all the ribbon show to the best advantage. While a few bows will have the ribbon folded so as to make a plain loop before it is plaited or gathered at the center, the great majority of bows should be made by plaiting single thicknesses of ribbon only. The shape to which the ends of the ribbon are cut usually marks the period of the bow, just as if it were labeled with the date at which it was made. For example, during one season ribbons will be scalloped; during another season, fish-tailed; during another season, cut on a long bias; while during still another season the ribbon will be cut very sharp and pointed. Great care should be exercised in properly trimming the ends of the ribbon before a bow is started.

In selecting ribbons for the following bows, care should be taken to purchase those which have well-finished selvages on both sides. Some of the cheaper varieties of ribbons are woven in wide pieces, which are then cut into strips. Consequently, ribbons of this kind have no selvage edges. Ribbons are brought out by the manufacturers in the new shades each season, and novelties in ribbons are being constantly placed on the market. If the bow to be made is to have the loop standing erect, the ribbon selected should be strong and firm.

BOWS MADE WITHOUT NEEDLE AND THREAD

Girdle Bow. Occasionally a good-looking bow can be made without the use of needle or thread. The girdle bow, shown completed in *Fig. 14*, belongs to this class.

Fig. 14

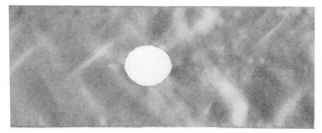

Fig. 15

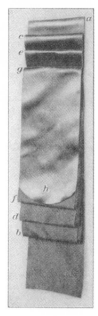

Fig. 16

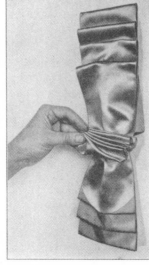

   (a)   *(b)*

Fig. 17

It is made of No. 50 ribbon, of which 3 yd. is required. At a point 8 in. from one end of the piece of ribbon cut a circular opening 1½ in. in diameter, as shown in *Fig. 15*. This can best be done by folding the ribbon lengthwise and then crosswise in the middle through the point where the center of the opening is to be, and then cutting a quarter-circle out of the corner of the folded material. Be careful not to cut the hole larger than 1½ in. in diameter, however. The ribbon is then ready to be folded so as to produce the loops.

Lay the ribbon on the top of a work table or a lap board, with the satin side down, and stretch it out smoothly. At a point 8 in. above the center of the hole cut in the ribbon, fold the ribbon back toward the bottom, making the first top loop *a, Fig. 16 (a)*. Draw the ribbon downwards a distance of 15 in. and turn it back to the top, forming the first bottom loop *b*. Draw the ribbon upwards a distance of 14 in. and turn it down to form the second top loop *c*. Draw the ribbon downwards a distance of 13 in. and turn it up to form the second bottom loop *d*. Draw the ribbon upwards 12 in. and turn it down to form the third top loop *e*. Draw the ribbon downwards 11 in. and turn it up to form the third bottom loop *f*. Finally draw the ribbon upwards 10 in. and turn it down to form the fourth top loop *g*. Then draw the ribbon downwards, cut it off even with the third bottom loop *f*, and trim the end *h* to a circular, or scalloped, form. These loops of ribbon may be pinned together from the back, so that they will not be liable to slip apart. The four upper loops will show the satin face of the ribbon and the three bottom loops will show the back of the ribbon.

Pick up the three bottom loops and the end *h, Fig. 16 (a)*, and draw them to one side so that the opening in the long end of the ribbon is uncovered, as in *(b)*. Squeeze the three loops and the rounded end together and push them through the hole, as shown in *Fig. 17 (a)*. Next, pick up the long end of the ribbon in which the hole is cut, and gather it into a series of plaits, as shown in *(b)*. Be careful to arrange the plaits so that each projects slightly above the one on top of it, as shown clearly in *Fig. 14*. Grasp the selvages at opposite ends of the plaits, bend the plaits back and around the bow, crushing the ribbon together at the center, and pin the selvage edges together firmly at the back. The bow is then finished, and appears as in the illustration. Such a bow as this is particularly effective at the waist line of the left side front or in the center back.

Tied Bows. The most intricately made bow is not always the most beautiful. Quite frequently the very simplest methods will produce creations of wondrous beauty. Much difficulty is experienced in plaiting narrow ribbons; therefore, better results may be obtained by employing other methods for making bows of narrow ribbon. The tied bow shown in *Fig. 18* is easy to make, but it requires the services of an assistant. Have a second person place her hands together, as shown in *Fig. 19*, with the forefingers extended stiffly and the remaining fingers doubled and braced together so as to hold the forefingers steady and about 4 in. apart.

Fig. 18

Loop a piece of No. 1, 3, or 5 ribbon, as desired, over the extended forefingers and cross the ends, as shown. Next, push the short end back and upwards behind the top of the looped ribbon and grasp the end as shown in *Fig. 20*. Draw the free ends forwards, as in *Fig. 21 (a),* taking care to have them crossed exactly at the center of the looped ends. Then tie a knot with the free ends, as indicated in *(b),* and draw the knot up tight around the middle of the loop. Finally, cut off the ends on the bias so that they are of equal lengths, and the bow will appear as in *Fig. 18*. Care must be taken, of course, to keep the satin face of the ribbon out.

In order to brace the forefingers in tying a bow of this kind, a block of wood 2 or 3 in. long and 1 in. wide may be held between the hands; or, if a large number of bows are to be made, and it is desired to have them all of the same size, two round, smooth sticks or pegs may be driven into holes in the work table, the holes being spaced so as to produce bows of the required size. Bows of the kind shown in *Fig. 18* are used on lingerie and children's dresses; also, they are extensively employed for trimming petticoats, corset covers, and other undergarments. If larger and fuller bows are desired, as, for

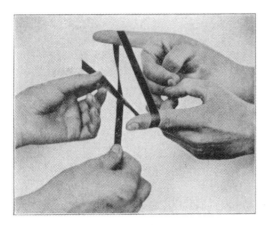

Fig. 19

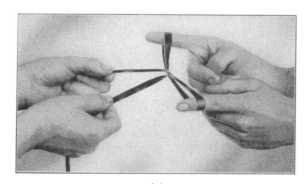

(a)

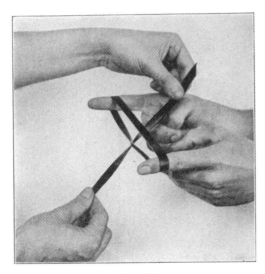

Fig. 20

(b)

Fig. 21

Fig. 22

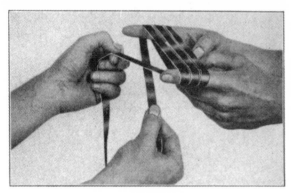

Fig. 23

example, the kind shown in *Fig. 22*, wrap the ribbon three times around the forefingers, as illustrated in *Fig. 23*, tie the knot over the three turns in the same manner as explained before, and cut off the ends on the bias and of equal lengths.

BOWS MADE WITH NEEDLE AND THREAD

Pump Bow. The easiest bow to make, as well as the simplest type used for tailored dresses, girdles, and children's coats, is the pump bow shown in *Fig. 24 (a)*. It is also used for bows on pumps and slippers, for a flat bow at the neck or on a belt, and for numerous other purposes. A heavy, firm ribbon is usually best for a tailored bow, as it holds in shape better than other ribbon and gives the substantial appearance characteristic of such a bow. However, the same plan may be worked out with a milliner's fold of silk or satin, giving a plain bow that is a little softer in appearance and, consequently, better adapted for use on a dress or a child's frock or coat. The size and position of such a bow depends considerably on the width and quality of material used. When it is to be sewed flat, have the stitch concealed near the end of each loop. Then put the

finger in the center loop and also each end loop and pull the bow up so that it presents a full, rounded appearance. Do not mash it down tightly.

The bow shown in *Fig. 24 (a)* is made of No. 5 grosgrain ribbon. Cut one piece of ribbon 6 in. long and another piece 3 in. long. Fold back both cut ends of the 6-in. piece so that they very nearly meet at the center and fasten them by stitching both securely, as shown in *(b)*. Lay this squarely across the middle of the 3-in. strip of ribbon, forming a cross, as in the illustration, and pin it in position. Lap both cut ends *a* and *b* over and sew them fast by overcasting, as shown in *(c)*. Be careful not to sew through all the thicknesses of the ribbon, but merely through the two overlapping pieces.

Rose Bow. Another fairly simple and easily constructed bow is the rose bow, shown in *Fig. 25*. Much time and practice should be given to making this bow, as it

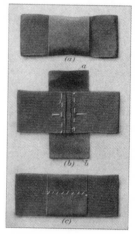

Fig. 24

Fig. 25

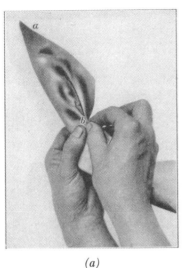 

(a)	*(b)*

Fig. 26

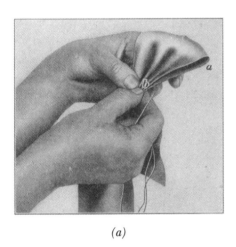 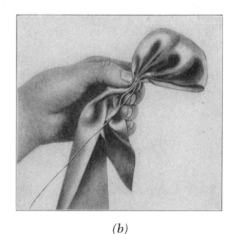

(a)	*(b)*

Fig. 27

contains all the fundamental operations used in making an endless variety of fashionable ribbon garnitures. It consists of seven loops of No. 40 ribbon tied together at the center, and requires 1½ yd. of ribbon. The first step in its construction is to cut the end of the ribbon on the bias, so as to form a long point, as shown at *a, Fig. 26 (a).* Then take the ribbon in the right hand and make plaits at *b* with the left hand, placing one plait directly on top of the other. These plaits should be very small and fine. After all the plaits have been made, hold them firmly between the thumb and forefinger of the left hand and fasten a thread in the selvage of the ribbon only. This is done to prevent the needle marks from showing in the body of the ribbon. After the thread has been fastened firmly to the selvage, wrap it tightly four or five times around the plaits directly above the thumb and forefinger, as shown in *(b),* and fasten the thread in the selvage of the ribbon again, thus finishing the foundation for the first half of the first loop. Do not break the thread.

The next step is shown in *Fig. 27 (a).* Turn the ribbon around so that the pointed end is down and start the second half of the first loop, holding the ribbon between the thumb and middle finger of the left hand and using the forefinger as a gauge for making the loop of the proper length. Hold the left forefinger stiffly in the air and draw the ribbon up over it, forming the loop *a.* Gather the ribbon into a number of fine plaits at *b,* directly over the place where the first plaits were made and tied. Draw the forefinger from under the top of the loop and grasp the loop over the plaits between the thumb and the forefinger, as shown in *(b).* Wrap the thread around the bottom of the loop, so that it not only will go over the outside of the second series of plaits, but will be in exactly the same place as the first wrapping of the thread. Then fasten the thread to the selvage edge of the ribbon as before.

When the first loop has been made, begin the second loop by drawing the ribbon over the forefinger in exactly the same manner as in making the first loop, in

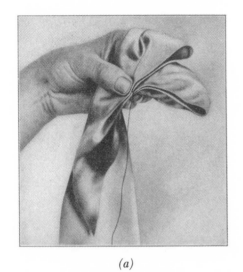

(a)

Fig. 30

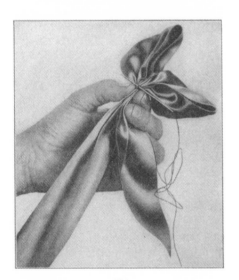

(b)

Fig. 28

Fig. 31

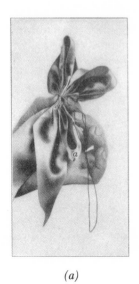

(a)

(b)

Fig. 29

Fig. 32

the manner indicated in *Fig. 28 (a)*. Take care to have the loops of the same length. Lay the selvage edge directly on top of the selvage of the first loop and plait as previously described. Wrap the thread firmly around the two loops and sew and fasten it to the selvage of the ribbon as shown in *(b.)* The reason for plaiting each single thickness of ribbon when the loop is being made, rather than plaiting two thicknesses at one time, is that the former method makes the ribbon show up to better advantage. This is illustrated clearly in the finished bow, *Fig. 25*. Not only do both surfaces *a* and *b* of each loop show plainly, but the plaiting causes the loop to open, as at *c*, so that the inside is visible, also. If the loop is folded first, and then both thicknesses are plaited, the loop will not stand open, and only the two faces will show.

When the second loop has been made and fastened, drop the first loop so that it lies beside the end of ribbon that was cut on the bias, as shown at *a, Fig. 29 (a)*. Grasp the partly completed bow at the center with the thumb and middle finger of the left hand, and use the forefinger as a guide in making the third loop. Make this loop in exactly the same manner as that followed in making the second loop, wrap it with thread, and fasten the thread at the selvage edge, as shown. Continue in this manner, dropping one loop down as each succeeding loop is made. This is done in order to keep all the wrappings of the thread directly in the center and to cover the wrappings on one loop by the wrappings of the thread on the next succeeding loop. The majority of well-balanced bows should have an uneven number of loops, such as five, seven, nine, eleven, thirteen, etc. This bow has seven, and the seven loops and one end are shown in *(b)*.

Next, turn the bow around so that the pointed end of the ribbon stands upright, as at *a, Fig. 30,* and divide the seven loops so that three lie beside the end *a* and four extend downwards, as shown. Grasp the uncut ribbon *b* in the left hand, draw it across the center of the bow, twisting it as at *c* and completely covering the threads that were wrapped around the plaits of the several loops. Wrap the twisted ribbon completely around the bow at the center, and in order to hold it in place, sew it to the back of the bow, as shown in *Fig. 31*. Stitch it first along one side as indicated by the position of the needle, and then along the other side, fastening it close to the point where the first loop was started. Finally, cut the other end of the ribbon on the bias to correspond to the shape of the end first cut, and draw it down so that it lies close to the first end, as shown in the completed bow, *Fig. 25*.

The rose bow may be used for a great number of purposes—for girdle and neck finishes, for ribbon-trimmed sleeves, the latter requiring very narrow, soft ribbon, for boas, for children's caps and dresses, as well as for millinery work. It is the style of bow that is invariably made to be placed on the bandeau of a hat, underneath the brim, the pointed ends either lying close to the brim or extending down and fitting close to the hair.

Full-Blown Ribbon Bow. The bow shown completed in *Fig. 32* is known as a full-blown ribbon bow because there is no knot in the center, and after the bow is finished it presents a full, rounded appearance similar to the half of a globe. Thin, light-weight, satin-faced ribbon is the proper material to be used for this bow. Either No. 16 or No. 22 ribbon should be used, and 2¼ yd. is required. Lay the ribbon on top of a work table or a lap board, cut one end on the bias to a pronounced point, measure off 12 in. from this point, and make a mark on the selvage edge of the ribbon. Measure off 12 in. from this mark and make another mark, and 12 in. farther on do the same thing, continuing until six marks are made on the selvage of the ribbon. These marks should not be more than ⅛ in. long; or they may be only dots made by the point of a pencil.

At the first mark on the selvage, 12 in. from the pointed end of the ribbon, make a series of plaits across the ribbon, one on top of another. When they are made, tie a knot in the plaited part and be sure that the center of this knot is exactly over the mark on the selvage. To insure that the mark will be at the center of the knot, a pin may be thrust through the selvage at the mark, as shown in *Fig. 33 (a)*. This illustration also shows the plaitings made in the ribbon. Grasp the ribbon as

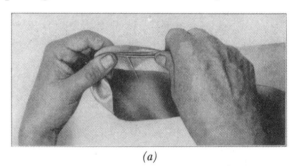

(a)

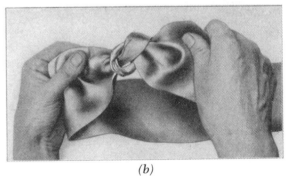

(b)

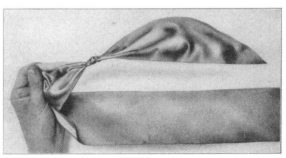

(c)

Fig. 33

shown, make a loop of the plaited part, slip the short end through the loop, and draw it out, pulling the ribbon into a knot, as shown in *(b)*. Adjust the position of the knot so that it will come directly at the mark, and remove the pin from the selvage, if a pin has been used. Then pull on the opposite ends of the ribbon and draw the knot very tight, as shown in *(c)*. The finished knot should be no thicker than a lead pencil and the mark on the selvage should be wholly concealed in the center of it. Make the same kind of knot, in exactly the same way, at the second mark on the selvage, and continue until six equally spaced knots have been made in the ribbon. The ribbon is then ready to be gathered into the form of the bow shown in *Fig. 32*.

Midway between the end of the ribbon and the first knot, along the lower selvage edge, gather the ribbon together in a number of fine plaits, as shown between the thumb and forefinger of the right hand in *Fig. 34 (a)*, making a plaited point about ¾ in. long. Crush these plaits together, wrap a thread around them, and sew the thread fast to the selvage, thus holding the plaits firmly; but do not break off the thread. Midway between the first and second knots plait a second point in the same

edge of the ribbon. Lay this bunch of plaits directly on top of the first bunch made, wrap them together with the thread and fasten the thread in the selvages. The bow at this stage will appear as in *(b)*, in which the two points of ribbon that have been fastened together are shown between the thumb and forefinger of the right hand. The first knot will be at the outer end of a loop formed in the ribbon. Midway between the second and third knots, gather the edge into a third point and attach it to the others, and continue in this manner until six loops have been made. Then trim off the other end of the ribbon on the bias to correspond to the end first trimmed, and the bow is completed.

Bows of the form illustrated in *Fig. 32*, when made of soft, narrow ribbon, are particularly well adapted for trimming dresses for children and misses. They are likewise suitable for corsage bows, especially in violet color of No. 3 ribbon. When made of narrower ribbon, the distance between the knots should be shorter than 12 in. With a No. 5 ribbon the distance between the marks for the knots should be not greater than 5 in. and with No. 7 or No. 9 ribbon it should be not greater than 9 in. As many loops as may be desired can be made.

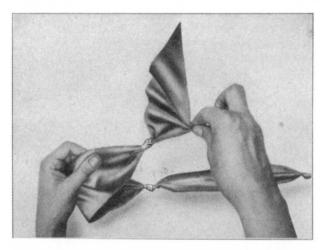

(a)

(b)

Fig. 34

Fig. 35

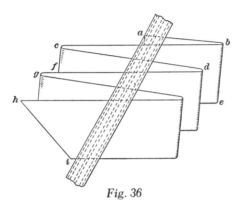

Fig. 36

Zigzag Bow. The bow shown in *Fig. 35*, known as the zigzag bow, may, if made of wide ribbon, be used at the center front or the center back of dresses or kimonos as a finish for high waist lines, as well as for the front of nightgowns. If it is made of narrow ribbon, it makes a pleasing sleeve or shoulder bow. The zigzag bow shown in the illustration is made of No. 80 ribbon, of which 3⅛ yd. is required. Such a bow is made as follows:

Cut the end of the ribbon square and lay it on the top of the work table, as at *a, Fig. 36*. Draw the ribbon to the right for a distance of 9 in., to the point *b*, and at this point turn the ribbon back and draw it to the left for a distance of 18 in., to the point *c*. Pin the ribbon to the table at both of these points to prevent the ribbon from slipping. The piece of ribbon drawn to the left should not be directly over the 9-in. end, but should run downwards in a slanting direction so that the selvage of the ribbon will be about 1 in. below the corner *a* of the first strip, where it crosses the cut end of the ribbon. Now fold the ribbon back to the right for a distance of 16 in., to the point *d*, and fold it again to the left. This fold *d* should be placed on top of the preceding strip and at about the middle of the strip. As the length *c d* is only 16 in., and *b c* is 18 in., the point *d* will be about 2 in. from the end *b e* of the preceding strip. Draw the ribbon downwards to the left for a distance of 18 in., as before, so that one-half of the preceding strip will show from *c* to *f*, and so that the corner *g* will extend beyond the point *f* for a distance of 2 in. Again draw the ribbon 16 in. to the right, fold it, and draw it again to the left for

a distance of 18 in., to *h*. It will be found by this method of arranging the ribbon that the selvage of the ribbon is running in a zigzag manner. The piece of ribbon should be cut on the bias from *h* to *i*, as shown. As these folds require 2⅝ yd., there will be ½ yd. of ribbon left.

The remaining ½ yd. of ribbon should be cut through the center lengthwise, and one of the pieces thus obtained should be laid diagonally on top of the zigzag folds of ribbon as shown in *Fig. 36*. Pin this strip of ribbon to the zigzag folds, to hold it in position, and make three double rows of machine stitching, as indicated by the three pairs of dotted lines, the stitching to go through the extra piece of ribbon and also the zigzag folds. The first double row of stitching should be directly in the center of the cut piece and the other two at the edges of the piece. The stitching must be done from the bottom to the top of the bow in order that the presser foot of the machine will not turn up the upper selvage edges of the zigzag strips. After the pieces of ribbon have been sewed together, either push a piece of fine wire through each of the double rows of stitching or draw a firm small cord through them, and then push the ribbon tightly together on the wires or the cords. Draw the ends of each wire or cord together, fastening them so as to form a circle of each, with the cut piece of ribbon inside, thus completing the bow shown in *Fig. 35*. It will have three loops at one end and two loops and an end of ribbon at the other. These loops should be pulled in position and rounded at the ends so as not to have a flat appearance.

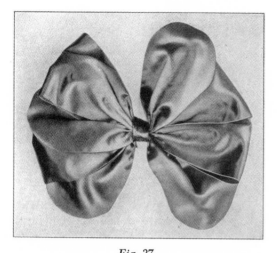

Fig. 37

Fig. 38

Fig. 39

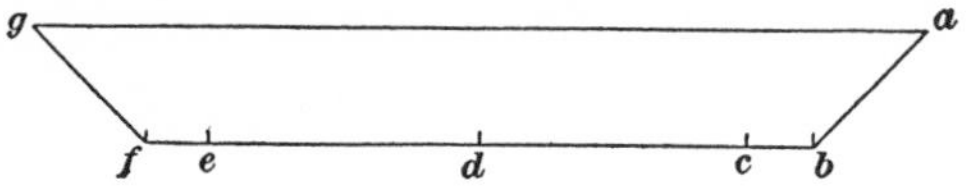

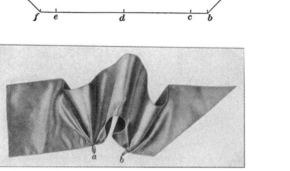

Fig. 40

Bat-Wing Bow. The bat-wing bow, illustrated in *Fig. 37*, requires 2⅛ yd. of No. 60 ribbon. Four pieces, each 18 in. long, are cut off and the remaining ⅛ yd. is used to form the center of the bow. Each 18-in. strip of ribbon is to be made into one loop and one end, the loop to be 6 in. long, requiring 12 in. of ribbon, and the end to be 6 in. long. Plait the ribbon across one end, placing one plait on top of the other, wrap thread around the plaits, and fasten the thread securely in the selvage of the ribbon. Twelve inches from this plaiting, make another row of plaits across the ribbon in exactly the same manner. Fold the ribbon over midway between the plaitings, place the first bunch of plaits on top of the last, and wrap both securely with the thread. Then cut the end of the ribbon to a rounded or semicircular form. Prepare the other three pieces in exactly the same manner, so that each has one 6-in. round end and one 6-in. loop.

After the four pieces have been properly prepared, lay them together, one just below the other, as in the illustration. Put the loops of two of the pieces to the left and the other two to the right, and sew the four pieces together at the center firmly and securely. The stitches that are used to fasten the pieces should next be covered with the remaining ⅛ yd. of ribbon. Fold this ribbon into a number of plaits, as shown, and sew the end of the ribbon at the back of the bow. Draw the plaits around the center of the bow; then turn the raw edge under and fasten it at the back.

This style of bow may be used as a girdle bow, and when made smaller it serves very well as a sleeve or shoulder bow. It is an exceptionally good bow for misses who braid their hair.

Show-All Bow. The show-all bow, illustrated in *Fig. 38*, requires 1¾ yd. of No. 60 ribbon. It is so named because almost all the ribbon on both sides shows in the completed bow. Fold over the end of the ribbon and cut it on a perfect bias, as shown at *a b*, *Fig. 39*. Lay the ribbon on the work table and make a mark *c* on the lower selvage edge with the point of a pencil, 2½ in. from the corner *b*. Eleven inches from this mark make another mark *d* on the bottom selvage edge and 11 in. farther on make another mark *e*. At a point *f* 2½ in. from the mark *e* the ribbon must be folded over and cut on the bias, as at *f g;* but this bias must run in an opposite direction to that at *a b*. From the remainder of the ribbon cut a second piece exactly like that just made, and mark it at corresponding points along the short selvage edge.

The two pieces of ribbon are now ready to be made up into the bow. Pick up the ribbon, and with the thumb and forefinger of the right hand bunch it at each of the points *c*, *d*, and *e*, *Fig. 39*, in the manner shown at *a* and *b*, *Fig. 40*. Wrap each bunch tightly with thread, so that each little tongue of ribbon is about ¾ in. long. Fasten the thread by sewing through the selvage. When the three tongues have been made, the ribbon for the left-hand side of the bow is ready. Prepare the ribbon for the right-hand side of the bow in exactly the same manner, bunching the ribbon at each of the three central marks, wrapping each bunch with thread, and fastening the thread securely. Next draw together the three tongues of ribbon on one piece and sew them together, forming the left-hand side of the bow. Do the same thing with the other piece, for the right-hand side. Lay the three tongues of ribbon on one half of the bow directly on top of the three tongues on the other half and wrap all securely with thread. From the remainder of the ribbon cut a piece 2½ in. long, lay it in folds, sew it to the joined tongues at the back, and wrap it over the center of the bow to cover the thread and the stitches. Turn the cut end of this piece under and sew it down to the tongues at the back. The bow will then present the finished appearance shown in *Fig. 38*.

The show-all bow is particularly well adapted for use where a small quantity of ribbon is to be shown to the best advantage. It is very attractive when made of No. 20 or No. 40 soft silk ribbon and used as a neck or a collar bow. It is also pleasing when developed in maline.

Moth, or Butterfly, Bow. The moth, or butterfly, bow, illustrated in *Fig. 41*, requires 3 yd. of No. 80 ribbon, which must be alike on both sides, and ½ yd. of No. 1 ribbon, the latter being sewed across the wider ribbon in order to outline the part of the bow that corresponds to the body of the moth. The baby ribbon may be of the same color as the wider ribbon, or of a contrasting color. The manner of arranging the wide ribbon to make this bow is illustrated in *Fig. 42*, which shows several folds. Begin by laying one end of the ribbon on the work table as at *a*. Draw the ribbon to the right, sloping downwards, for a distance of 7 in., or to *b*. At

this point fold it back on itself and draw it to the left, giving it a half-twist so as to cause it to slant downwards to the left, and also to bring the opposite side of the ribbon on top. Draw it down to the left and fold it back on itself at the point *c*, which should be just as far to the left of the center *d* as the point *b* is to the right of the center. Give the ribbon another half-twist, draw it down to the right, and continue as before, until four loops have been made on the right and three loops and an end on the left. After each loop has been made, pin it at the middle as shown. Cut the end on the bias, as shown at *e, Fig. 41*. Also, turn the corner *a, Fig. 42*, down under the folds of ribbon, as at *f, Fig. 41*. Observe that the loops are not laid directly on top of one another, but that each is 1 in. below the preceding one.

After the ribbon has been properly folded to produce four loops on the right side and three loops and a bias end on the left side, the bow is ready to be stitched. Pin the ribbon to hold it in position and lay on it two strips of No. 1 ribbon. These strips run up and down and should be 1 in. on each side of the center of the ribbon used to form the bow. Make a double row of machine stitching on each piece of baby ribbon by stitching along the selvage of each piece, sewing through the folded wider ribbon. Push a piece of lace wire between the two rows of stitching and underneath each strip of baby ribbon and shove the loops together, as shown at the center of the bow, *Fig. 41*. Draw the ends of the two wires at the top and at the bottom together and twist them tightly, after which push the twisted ends of the wires back under the bow. The twisting of the ends of the wire together at both top and bottom forms a hump in the center of the bow, or, in other words, makes the body of the moth.

The moth, or butterfly, bow is particularly well adapted as a finish for a girdle at the center back; likewise, it may be used as a kimono bow, being placed at the center back in Empire effect.

Fig. 41

Fig. 42

RIBBON ROSETTES
AND FLOWERS

ROSETTES

Rosettes in some form are used each season in some way and in some place as a garment decoration, especially on garments for children and on lingerie. The size and color of the ribbon employed for rosettes determines almost entirely the uses to which they may be put, as well as the number that may be used. If the rosettes are large and made of dark ribbon, seldom if ever is more than one employed; whereas, if they are small and made of light ribbon, they may be used in great number if desired.

Camera Rosette. The camera rosette, shown in *Fig. 43*,

Fig. 43

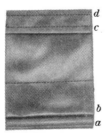

Fig. 44

requires 2⅔ yd. of No. 40 ribbon, which must be cut into ten strips, each 9½ in. long. Take one strip of the ribbon, measure off 3 in. from one end, and make a mark on the selvage. Measure ½ in. from this first mark and make a second mark; 2½ in. from the second mark make a third mark; 2 in. from the third mark make a fourth mark; ½ in. from the fourth mark make a fifth mark; and ½ in. from the fifth mark make a sixth mark. At the end of the ribbon from which the 3-in. space was marked off, turn under ⅛ in., as for making a hem. Place the folded edge of this hem directly even with the first mark on the selvage, at the back, and stitch the ribbon straight across from selvage to selvage, through the three thicknesses of ribbon, making what would be practically a 1½-in. hem at the end of the ribbon. The lower edge of this hem is shown at *a, Fig. 44*. Push the ribbon up so that the second mark is directly opposite the third mark and sew across from selvage to selvage, making a tuck 1¼ in. deep, as shown at *b*. Two inches from this row of stitching is the fourth mark. Push the ribbon together so that the fourth mark comes even with the fifth mark, and sew across from selvage to selvage, making a ¼-in. tuck, as shown at *c*. Turn the end of the ribbon under ¼ in. as if to make an ordinary hem, and stitch across from selvage to selvage at the sixth mark, as shown by the stitching at *d*. Be very careful to have all rows of stitching straight. Prepare the other nine pieces of ribbon in the same manner.

Take a piece of fine wire, bend back the end ¼ in., and flatten the loop with the pliers. Lay the ten pieces of ribbon down one beside another so that the wide hems are at the bottom and the narrow hems at the top. Push the wire through the ¼-in. hem at the top of each of the ten strips of ribbon, push the ribbon closely together, and draw the wire around in the form of a circle 1½ or 2 in. in diameter. Fasten the two ends of this wire together by twisting. Push a fine wire through each of the tucks *c, Fig. 44*, and after the ends of the wire have come together fasten them by twisting them together, making the outer circle at the center of the rosette, *Fig. 43*. This outer circle will be 2½ or 3 in. in diameter. Both circles should lie perfectly flat, and care should be taken to see that the wide hems overlap in the same direction around the rosette.

Fig. 45

Fig. 46

Fig. 47

Fig. 48

Fig. 49

Fig. 50

Camera rosettes made of black or dark grosgrain ribbon are particularly attractive for both skirt and waist ornaments on dark afternoon dresses, especially when used on nun tucks. They serve likewise as a finish for girdle ends, and when made small they are excellent collar and sleeve rosettes.

Pinwheel Rosette. The pinwheel rosette is shown completed in *Fig. 45 (a)*. It requires 1⅔ yd. of No. 40 ribbon, which is cut into twelve pieces of the shape shown in *(b)*. The length *a b* is 8¾ in. and the length *c d* is ½ in. To save material, the pieces should be cut with the long edge of one piece next the short edge of the adjoining piece. After the twelve pieces of ribbon have been cut to this shape, gather each piece across one bias end and along the ½-in. selvage. In making this gathering, hold the ribbon in the hand with the short length of selvage farthest from the body, and gather it from *b* to *d* and then from *d* to *c*. The gathers should be drawn up so that the gathered edge will not be longer than 1 in., and the piece will appear as in *(c)*. Fasten the thread securely, and prepare each of the remaining strips in the same manner. Cut a small circular piece of buckram 1½ in. in diameter and cover it with a scrap of silk; the first bias corner that is cut from the ribbon may be used for this purpose. Sew the gathered parts of the prepared pieces to this foundation, beginning at the center and radiating the pieces so that the points of ribbon will be equidistant from one another.

Pinwheel rosettes are particularly good when several are grouped on a garment, being very effective when two-toned ribbon is used; that is, one color on one side and a different color on the other.

Turbine Rosette. The turbine rosette shown in *Fig. 46* requires 2¾ yd. of No. 9 ribbon. Start at the end of the ribbon and measure off 4½ in. Either make a pencil mark at this point or put in a pin. At a distance of 3 in. from this mark make a second mark on the selvage; 4½ in. farther on make a third mark; 3 in. farther on make another mark; and so continue to mark off alternate distances of 4½ in. and 3 in. to the end of the ribbon. Gather the ribbon quite near the selvage edge over the 4½-in. space and draw it up so that it is not more than 1 in. in length. Now, skip the 3-in. space and gather the next 4½-in. space, drawing the ribbon up so that the gathering thread will not be more than 1 in. in length. Fasten the thread securely, skip the next 3-in. space, gather the next 4½-in. space, and so continue to the end of the ribbon. A part of the ribbon thus prepared is shown in *Fig. 47.* If pins are used as markers, they should be removed as the gathering is proceeded with.

After the whole of the 2¾ yd. of ribbon has been gathered at intervals of 3 in., as just described, it is ready to be formed into a rosette. To begin, fold the first 3-in. plain part under the 4½-in. gathered part at the end of the ribbon, as shown in *Fig. 48,* and stitch the selvages together at the point *a,* where they cross. The plain part forms the back, the 4½-in. gathered part forms the face of one leaf, and the point *a* is at the center of the rosette. To form the next leaf, lay the second 4½-in. gathered part so that it overlaps the first, as shown in *Fig. 49.* Then fold the second 3-in. plain part under and inwards, as in *Fig. 50,* and stitch the selvage fast at the center *a.* Continue in the same manner to fasten the remaining leaves until the rosette is completed, as in *Fig. 46.*

Rosettes of this sort are particularly well adapted for garments for misses and children.

Petal-and-Ruffle Rosette. The form of rosette shown in *Fig. 51* consists of three rows of petals surrounding a center of ruffles, the whole being attached to a buckram cabochon° 3¾ in. in diameter. The petals, which are forty-nine in number, require 3⅓ yd. of No. 9 ribbon, and the ruffled center requires 1 yd. of the same width of ribbon. The pieces for the making of the petals are cut to the shape shown in *Fig. 52,* measuring 3¾ in. along the long selvage edge *a b* and 1 in. along the short selvage edge *c d.* Stitch each piece along close to the edge from *b* to *d, Fig. 52,* then from *d* to *c,* and finally from *c* to *a;* then draw up the thread so that the stitched edges will be gathered into a space of ¾ in., as shown in *Fig. 53.* When all the petals have been prepared, cut the remaining yard of ribbon lengthwise in the center, sew the two pieces end to end, and run a gathering thread along the cut edge, as shown in *Fig. 54,* making the ruffle that forms the center.

Use a buckram cabochon foundation 3¾ in. in diameter, cover it with sheet wadding,† and then with a piece of silk. To it sew the forty-nine petals, beginning

°See Publisher's Note.
†Quilt batting.

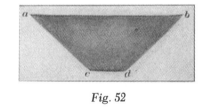

Fig. 52

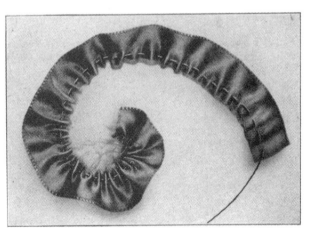

Fig. 53

Fig. 51

Fig. 54

with the outer row, which contains eighteen petals. The second petal should be set on so that its edge will overlap the first petal almost to the middle; the third petal should overlap the second to the same extent; and the remaining petals should be arranged in a similar manner. The second row, which contains seventeen petals, is sewed fast ½ in. inside the first row; and the third row, containing fourteen petals, is attached ½ in. inside the second row. After the petals are fastened to the cabochon, the ruffle is sewed in a spiral so as to hide the stitches on the inner row of petals and fill up the entire center of the rosette.

Rosettes of this kind are used on dresses for misses and children as waist-line and sleeve or shoulder finishes, and frequently one is placed on nun tucks in a skirt, at the side or the center front. Ribbon petals are quite frequently used to form edges and borders for collar and sleeve finishes; also, they are used for trimming bands and baby bonnets. Smaller rosettes may be made by using narrower ribbon, smaller cabochons, and fewer petals.

RIBBON FLOWERS AND FRUITS

Although ribbon is used extensively in the making of bows, rosettes, and other trimmings, it may also be worked up into clever imitations of fruits and flowers. Such ornaments or trimmings as these find a varied use in connection with garments, many times serving to add just that something which will serve to increase or enhance the appearance of a dress, a gown, or a suit. The ornaments or trimmings that follow are all practical and will be the means of unfolding ideas that can be utilized to advantage in making other trimmings of a similar nature.

Cabochon Foundations. * In the making of flowers and various other ornaments, whether of ribbon or of other materials, cabochon foundations will be found very useful. A cabochon foundation is merely a small piece of buckram pressed into a dome or a similar shape. A number of cabochon foundations of various shapes and sizes are shown in *Fig. 55*, those in *(a)* being of white buckram and those in *(b)* of black buckram. In *(a)*, the two foundations at *a* and *b* are shown with their rough edges, just as they appear when they are purchased. Before they are used, the rough edges are trimmed off, and they then appear as at *c* and *d*. The foundations at *e* and *f* are trimmed, ready to be used. After the rough edge has been trimmed off, the bottom edge is wired with a piece of fine wire, using overcast stitches, to hold the foundation to its shape. The cabochon foundation is then covered with a scrap of silk, and it is ready to be used as the center of a flower or some other ornament.

Ribbon Grapes. In *Fig. 56* is illustrated a bunch of imitation grapes made from pieces of ribbon and

*See Publisher's Note.

milliner's tie wire, combined with a bit of foliage as a background. The bunch consists of six large grapes and seven small ones. For the large grapes, No. 16, and for the small ones No. 12 ribbon is sometimes used, but if it is not convenient to use ribbon, scraps of satin, silk, or

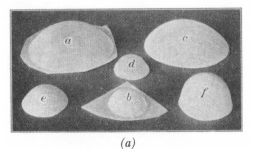

(a)

Fig. 55

Fig. 56

Fig. 57

Fig. 58

Fig. 59

velvet may be advantageously employed. Cut six circular pieces each 2¼ in. in diameter and, for the small ones cut seven circles each 1⅞ in. in diameter. Turn under the raw edge of each circular piece and run a gathering thread around it, as shown in *Fig. 57*, which illustrates the appearance of the back, or wrong side, of a circular piece of ribbon. The circles form the outer coverings, corresponding to the skins of the grapes. The centers, or insides, of the grapes are made of cotton wadding.*

From a piece of sheet wadding† cut seven circular pieces each 2¼ in. in diameter and lay them one on top of another. Draw the cut edges down and under, press with the fingers, and work the wadding into a firm round ball. When the ball has been properly rounded, loop thread around it to hold it in its rounded form. This ball makes the center for one of the large grapes. Take a piece of silk-covered tie wire 8 in. long, lay its middle point on top of the ball of wadding, draw the ends down around and under the ball, and twist them together tightly. Over the ball stretch the circle of silk shown in *Fig. 57*, drawing up the gathering thread and fastening it securely around the twisted wires beneath the ball. This operation finishes one of the large grapes, as shown in *Fig. 58*. The remaining five large grapes are made in exactly the same way, each requiring seven pieces of wadding. Each of the small grapes, however, requires six pieces of wadding 1⅞ in. in diameter, and is covered with one of the gathered circular pieces of ribbon of the same diameter. The small grapes are made in exactly the same way as the large ones.

When the grapes have been made as just described, gather the ends of the tie wires together in such a way as to make the grapes assume the form of a cluster, wider at the top and pointed at the bottom, as shown in *Fig. 56*. The tendrils, shown as spirals of wire, are made by wrapping pieces of silk-covered fine wire in a spiral on

*Quilt batting.

†Because today's polyester quilt batting is generally thicker than the cotton batting available in the 1920s, you will probably need fewer circles for each grape.

a round lead pencil. Fasten the upper ends of the tendrils to the tie wires that suspend the grapes, but hide the fastenings under the large grapes at the top of the cluster. The small grapes should be placed at the bottom, and the wires can be bent so as to spread them in the form of a natural cluster. The foliage can be purchased at any store dealing in millinery merchandise, and may be attached to the grapes by twisting its wire stem with the tie wires. Grape clusters of this kind may be made in natural colors by choosing the proper shades of ribbon; however, it is permissible to make them of any desired color of ribbon to harmonize with the gown with which they are to be worn. Grapes made of white satin with white foliage and white wires are particularly effective as a trimming on white dresses, especially those for evening wear.

Ribbon Daisies. The ribbon daisy shown in *Fig. 59* is made of satin baby-ribbon petals fastened at the center to a cabochon foundation ornamented with French knots, the whole being attached to suitable foliage. For making this daisy, use No. 1 ribbon, commonly called baby ribbon. There are 36 petals, each of which requires 4½ in. of ribbon, so that the total length of ribbon needed is 36 × 4½ = 162 in., or 4½ yd. Cut the 4½ yd. of ribbon into 36 pieces, each 4½ in. long. Lay each piece on the work table or the lap board and make a

Fig. 60

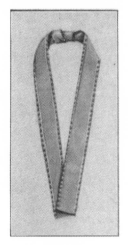

Fig. 61

Fig. 62

pencil mark at its middle point, or 2¼ in. from either end. Tie a knot in each piece of ribbon, directly at the center, where the mark is made, and draw the knot tight, so that the piece appears as in *Fig. 60*. The pencil mark should be wholly concealed in the center of the knot. Next prepare the cabochon foundation* that is to form the center of the daisy. Use the low, flat kind shown at *c, Fig. 55 (a)*, cut it down to a diameter of 1¼ in., and bind the edge with wire. Over it lay a circle of wadding of the same diameter, to act as a padding, and over the wadding stretch a scrap of silk of the same color as the ribbon used to form the petals. Sew the silk covering to the cabochon foundation, taking care to have it lie smooth.

Sew the petals to the cabochon foundation along the outer edge, but on the upper, or covered, surface. Take each of the 4½-in. pieces, which have been knotted at the center, and lay the ends one on top of the other, as in *Fig. 61*, taking care to have the right side of each half of the piece facing upwards. Sew this petal fast to the cabochon foundation by stitching through the two overlapped ends. Put on the next petal close to the first, and in the same way, and so continue until a row of petals has been sewed on all around the edge of the cabochon center. Then sew a second row directly on top of the first row. Each row, of course, should contain 18 petals, or half the total number used.

Use yellow rope silk† to make the center of the daisy,

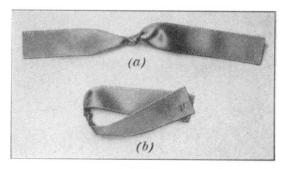

Fig. 63

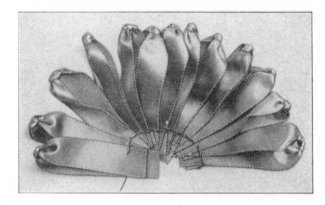

Fig. 64

*See Publisher's Note.
†Use ¹⁄₁₆″-wide ribbon or pearl cotton.

Fig. 65

shown in *(b)*, thus forming the separate petals. Place the fourteen petals, one slightly overlapping the other, as shown in *Fig. 64,* and backstitch them together in a half-circle. When the stitching is finished, bend the half-circle into a circle, with the last loop lapped under the first loop, and sew them together. A small bunch of stamens, which can be either purchased or made, is wrapped around with the thread to hold it securely in position and fastened down in the center of the flower. The flower may now be mounted on a piece of heavy wire 5 in. long, which should be covered with a green rubber tube,* or it may be sewed flat to a garment or to a girdle or a belt.

Ribbon Chrysanthemum. The ribbon chrysanthemum shown in *Fig. 65* may be made of petals of the same kind and size as those used in the construction of the daisy shown in *Fig. 62;* however, the chrysanthemum requires 9¼ yd. of No. 2 ribbon, as there are 74 petals like that shown in *Fig. 63 (b).* Prepare a buckram cabochon foundation† 2 in. in diameter, cover it with a single thickness of wadding,‡ and over that sew a scrap of silk of a color to match the ribbon petals. Then sew the petals to the cabochon center, beginning with the inner row. Lay a 5-cent piece directly in the center of the cabochon, and around its edge sew the first row of petals with their knotted ends pointing inwards toward the center of the flower. When the first row is sewed fast, remove the coin, as it is used only as a gauge to produce a round center. Sew the second row of petals in a circle at a distance of ¼ in. back of the first row, the third row ¼ in. back of the second row, and the fourth row on the edge of the cabochon. The fourth row should be sewed on so that the cut ends of the petals will be doubled over the edge of the cabochon and should be fastened on with overcast-stitches. This makes the flower flat at the back when the petals are pressed outwards so as to cover and conceal the stitches by which they are held fast. This flower may be either mounted on a wire or sewed flat. It is well adapted for use as a corsage bouquet when combined with foliage.

Full-Blown Rose. Flowers made of ribbon may be used at almost any time of the year and in many ways. The colors should be selected to harmonize with the season as nearly as possible. Possibly no other ribbon flower finds greater use than roses, for they fit in admirably with nearly all garments for women and children. In *Fig. 66* (page 28) is shown a full-blown rose made of ribbon and artificial foliage. To begin such a rose, cut a piece of heavy wire 5 in. in length, straighten it, and at the top fasten a small bunch of stamens, using eight or ten stamens doubled and tied around the wire with a thread, as shown in *Fig. 67.* This wire forms the stem of the rose, as well as the center on which the petals are mounted.

or, if it is to represent a brown-eyed Susan, use a rich, warm brown. Thread the rope silk into a darning needle or an embroidery needle and fill the center entirely full with a number of French knot-stitches, as shown in *Fig. 59,* covering and hiding the ends of the petals. Sew a piece of heavy wire across the back of the cabochon center of the flower and over the wire slip a piece of green rubber tube to form the stem.* Fasten the flower to a cluster of leaves. As fashion permits the use of foliage altogether different from that which might be found with a natural flower, it is possible to create and construct very novel conceits by using almost any kind of foliage desired. The petals may all be made of one solid color, or three or four colors that harmonize may be used. When made small, this is an attractive ornament for the shoulder of a gown or the lapel of a coat. Larger ones may be used at a girdle joining, especially at the left-side front. No. 1 velvet ribbon is very attractive for this daisy, but if such material is used it should be made on a smaller cabochon and a larger number of petals employed—usually a 1-in. cabochon with 42 petals. Such a garniture is very attractive for a fur piece.

Another style of daisy, made with stamens instead of the usual cabochon center, is shown completed in *Fig. 62.* This flower requires 1¾ yd. of No. 2 ribbon. Cut fourteen pieces of ribbon each 4½ in. long and tie a hard knot exactly in the center of each piece, as shown in *Fig. 63 (a).* Draw the ends of the piece together, right side up, the left overlapping the right, and sew them as

*See Publisher's Note.

*See Publisher's Note.
†See Publisher's Note.
‡Quilt batting.

Fig. 66

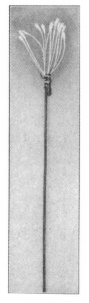

Fig. 67

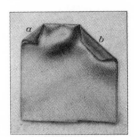

Fig. 68

The rose shown in *Fig. 66* requires 2¾ yd. of No. 12 ribbon, which is cut into pieces of different lengths and sewed to form the petals. Cut eight pieces each 4 in. long, eight pieces each 4½ in. long, and five pieces each 5 in. long, making twenty-one pieces that will be used for the petals. Take one of the 4-in. pieces and fold it in the middle, crosswise, with the right side out. Fold one doubled corner over to a width of less than ½ in.; then fold it again and hold the double fold lightly between the thumb and the forefinger. The first fold is shown on one corner at *a, Fig. 68,* and the second on the other corner at *b.* The double fold must be held in place by stitching through from the wrong side of the ribbon. Therefore, spread apart the two thicknesses forming the petal, still holding the double fold between the thumb and the forefinger, and take two or three backstitches, sewing through into the double fold so as to hold it securely. Be careful, however, to see that these stitches do not go completely through the double roll and show on the face of the ribbon. The wrong side of the petal, when turned out, is shown in *Fig. 69 (a)*, with the backstitches that hold one double fold in place. The front of the same piece is shown in *(b)*.

After one corner of the petal has been doubled over and stitched fast as shown in *Fig. 69*, the other corner must be treated in the same way and the petal will then appear as in *Fig. 70 (a)*. The second doubled corner is held by stitching through from the inside, as before, and the view *(b)* shows how the inside of the petal looks when the two parts are separated. The stitching that holds the corners can easily be seen at the center. The thread used for sewing down the first corner is drawn across the ribbon and used for sewing the second corner, thus doing away with the necessity of cutting off the thread and making a second knot. In the same manner, fold the remainder of the 4-in. pieces, roll down the corners, and stitch them in place. Do the same with the eight 4½-in. pieces and the five 5-in. pieces. The result will be twenty-one petals of the form shown in *Fig. 70 (a)*.

Before the petals are ready to be fastened to the central stem they must be plaited at the bottom, so as to cup them, or cause them to assume the curved shape of natural rose petals. The manner of doing this is very clearly shown in *Fig. 71*, in which *(a)* is a front view of the finished petal and *(b)* a back view. Make a deep plait at the lower, or cut, end of the petal and stitch it down firmly. Do this with each of the twenty-one petals, and then lay them aside, the eight short ones in one row, the eight medium-sized ones in another row, and the five large ones in a third row, so that they will not become mixed.

The petals, after they have been cupped by plaiting, are ready to be attached to the stem to form the rose. Take one of the small petals and wrap it around the top of the stem, very nearly covering the stamens. Sew it to the wire by wrapping the thread around several times and fastening it securely, as shown in *Fig. 72 (a)*. Put on the second petal directly facing the first one, so that its inner, or cupped, side will very nearly cover the stamens on the other side, as in *(b)*. Attach this petal to the wire by wrapping the thread around at the bottom and fastening it securely, the same as the first. Put on the third petal so that it is at the side of the first two and covers the opening between them. In order to give the rose a full, rounded appearance, the top of the third petal should be just a trifle lower than the tops of the first two. Sew the fourth petal at the other side of the first two, directly opposite the third petal, and at the same height as the third. At this stage four of the small petals are in place on the stem. Sew on the remaining four small petals, placing them so as to overlap the four openings between the first four petals.

Next take the eight medium-sized petals and sew them together side by side in pairs, producing four double petals, which must then be attached to the wire stem by being wrapped and sewed with the thread. The bottoms, or cut ends, of the double petals should be bunched together tightly, so as to cause the upper ends of the petals to straighten out and cup properly. After the four double petals have been attached to the stem, sew the five large petals on the outside of the others, gathering their ends closely to the wire. Then hold the rose in one hand and push the forefinger down, in, and around all of the different petals in order to cup them properly and to bend them into position, and thus give the rose its shape. The rose is then ready to have the foliage added.

Tear up some old artificial flowers that have become faded, crushed, or soiled so as to be unfit for further use, because there are certain parts that can be used for finishing the ribbon rose. A small star-shaped piece of green muslin will be found on the old flower, and this should be pushed on the wire stem and pressed up close against the bottom of the rose. Also, there will be found on the old flower a small green wax cup.* Remove this and push it on the wire stem to finish the bottom of the rose. If no old flowers are at hand, the star-shaped pieces may be cut from a piece of firm green silk, preferably taffeta; such pieces should be about ½ to ¾ in. in diameter. Also, the wax cups may be purchased at a millinery supply house. Cover the heavy wire with a piece of green rubber tubing,† which may likewise be purchased at a millinery supply house, and the rose is finished. Surround the rose thus made with a cluster of rose foliage and the garniture is ready to wear. This flower, if worn at the bust or the belt, is a beautiful finish for an evening gown or a dancing frock.

*These cups are now made of plastic.
†See Publisher's Note.

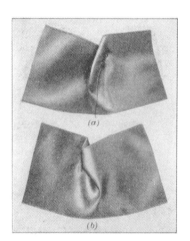

Fig. 69

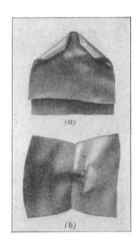

Fig. 70

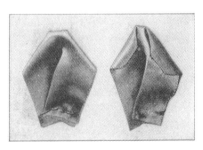

Fig. 71

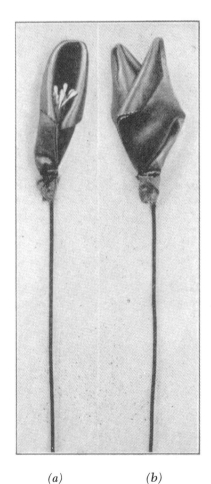

(a)   (b)

Fig. 72

Fig. 73

Fig. 74

Rosebuds. Small rosebuds in combination with foliage, as shown in *Fig. 73*, form a very charming trimming. The three buds shown require ¼ yd. of No. 50 ribbon to form the centers and ⅔ yd. of No. 5 ribbon to form the petals. Take the ¼-yd. piece of No. 50 ribbon and from it cut three pieces on the bias, each measuring 1½ in. on the selvage, or from *a* to *b*, *Fig. 74 (a)*. To make one of the centers, fold one of these bias pieces along the middle, as shown in *(b)*, with the right side out, and then wrap it around the end of a piece of fine wire 5 in. long, as shown in *(c)*. Continue wrapping until it is wound on the wire and then wrap it with thread and stitch it fast, as in *(d)*. If the center appears too thick and bulky when the whole bias piece is wrapped on the wire, the end may be cut off after three turns have been wound on the wire. To make the petals, cut the ⅔-yd. piece of No. 5 ribbon into twelve pieces, each 2 in. long. Fold these across the middle, right side out. Turn down the corners of each piece, as shown in *(e)*, stitch them fast from the inside, as previously explained, and then make a plait at the bottom, to cause the petal to assume a cupped form.

Make the remaining petals in exactly the same manner.

Four of the petals are needed for each bud. Take the center and its stem, as shown in *Fig. 74 (d)*, place a petal against it, with the turned-down corners outside, and attach the petal to the center by wrapping with thread and sewing. Place the next petal at the side of the first, the third at the side of the second, and the fourth at the side of the third and attach them all by wrapping them securely to the wire and sewing them fast. Next, slip a star-shaped piece of green cloth on the wire and press it up close to the satin petals, after which slip on the green wax cup° and cover the wire with a rubber stem.† Make the remaining buds in exactly the same manner as the first. The three buds may now be mixed with foliage, as in *Fig. 73*, or used in connection with the rose, as desired.

°Use a green plastic cup.
†See Publisher's Note.

Wild Rose. The wild rose shown completed in *Fig. 75* is made from five strips of No. 9 ribbon, each 3¼ in. long. Fold each strip crosswise in the middle, with the satin surfaces out. Hold it between the thumb and forefinger of one hand, close to the crease or fold at the top and with the other hand take a needle and push the corner down into the fold, as shown at *a, Fig. 76 (a)*. Do the same thing at the other corner. Then sew the selvage edges together at the points *a* and *b*, view *(b)*, using the *tie-stitch*. This stitch is made by pushing the needle through the selvages and drawing it up until the knot is within 1½ or 2 in. of the ribbon. The two ends of thread are then tied together and the thread is clipped off close to the knot. At the bottom of the petal make two plaits, the one from the right-hand side plaiting toward the center and the one from the left-hand side plaiting toward the center, as shown. This will produce the cupped effect necessary to make the petal.

To make the center of the rose, take a wooden button mold° ½ in. in diameter, cover it with a small square scrap of yellow velvet, pulling the four points together at the back, and wrap tightly with three or four wrappings of thread sewed securely. To this button mold at the back sew a number of stamens all the way around and spread them out. Just below where the stamens are sewed to the velvet sew the first petal, then the second, the third, the fourth, and the fifth, each petal slightly overlapping the preceding one. To the bunch of harmonizing velvet at the back fasten a wire 4 or 5 in. long, which should be covered with a rubber stem.† When the wild rose is attached to foliage it will appear like the finished ornament shown in *Fig. 75*. A small circle of buckram‡ the size of the bottom of a thimble may be used instead of the button mold, but it must first be covered with one or two thicknesses of sheet wadding.

°Use an aluminum button mold, available in notions departments.
†See Publisher's Note.
‡Use heavy interfacing or needlepoint canvas.

Fig. 75

(a)   *Fig. 76*   *(b)*

Fig. 77

Rapid Rose. The rapid rose shown in *Fig. 77* is so called because the ribbon that forms the petals is in one continuous strip, and is not cut into separate lengths. The making of the rose is therefore greatly hastened, inasmuch as the strip is simply wound around a center. One yard of No. 16 ribbon is required to make the rapid rose. The center is constructed of tissue paper. Cut a piece of tissue paper 8 in. long and 4 in. wide and fold it crosswise and lengthwise so that it measures 4 in. by 2 in. and has four thicknesses. Set the center of the folded piece on the end of the forefinger, draw the ends down, and wrap them around the forefinger. Slip the paper off the finger and it will be found to have the shape of a nipple. Untwist one fold of the paper, and under it lay one end of the ribbon on the bias. Fold the end of the ribbon in under and twist the paper back into its former shape. The ribbon put on in this manner forms a lining for the cup, as well as an outside covering. The tissue-paper center is completely enclosed by the ribbon and does not show when the rose is finished.

Fasten a thread at the bottom and wrap it several times around, crushing the ribbon tightly at the bottom of the center of the rose. Pull the ribbon up and away from where it has been fastened, so as to form the cupped petal, the first one to be made. Plait the ribbon in a circular form, as is clearly shown by the line of creases *a b c, Fig. 78*. When the ribbon is plaited as indicated by these wrinkles, and gathered close around the bottom of the rose, the part of the ribbon at *d* will form a cupped petal. Wrap the thread around the plaits and fasten it securely. Now push the ribbon forwards, plait it as before, and pull in the second petal so that its edge overlaps the preceding one. Continue in this manner until all the petals have been made. Then fasten the rose to a piece of heavy wire that is covered with a rubber stem.* Some practice will doubtless be required in plaiting and arranging the petals before this rose can be made satisfactorily; therefore, it is advisable to cut a strip of muslin 2½ in. wide and 1 yd. in length and to practice the making of this rose until the finished work resembles a half-blown natural rose. When sufficient expertness has been obtained in this manner, the rose can be quickly made with ribbon, as described.

*See Publisher's Note.

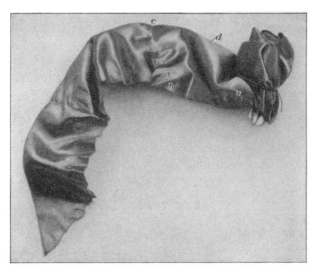

Fig. 78

Tiny Roses. Each of the tiny roses shown in *Fig. 79* requires a little less than 4 in. of No. 60 ribbon cut on the bias. Cut off the corner of the ribbon to make a perfect bias, measure 2 in. along the selvage, and cut the 2 in. off on the bias. Fold this 2-in. piece so that the two bias cut edges are even and gather it along the bottom, or near the cut edges. Draw up the gathering thread, wrap the piece around the end of the finger to form the center of the flower, and then wrap the thread around tightly and fasten it. Cut on the bias another strip of ribbon measuring 1¾ in. on the selvage edge, fold it so that the two cut edges come together, and make a zigzag running-stitch from one end of the ribbon to the other, making five zigzag figures, as in *Fig. 80*. Draw the thread tightly so that the ribbon will take the form shown in *Fig. 81*. In this illustration the unnecessary part of the ribbon inside the row of running-stitches is cut off from *a* to the middle, the other half being left just as it would appear after the thread is drawn up. The unnecessary part of the ribbon, however, should be cut off all along the row of running-stitches. After this has been done, draw the strip of five small petals around the base of the center already made, and sew it securely in place, making one of the finished flowers shown in *Fig. 79*.

Tiny roses of this sort are mixed with small foliage and used for trimming evening gowns, children's frocks, dancing and boudoir caps, etc. They may also be made of scraps of silk cut to the proper size and shape.

Fig. 79

Fig. 80

Fig. 81

Ribbon Violets. A piece of No. 1 ribbon 16 in. long is required for making each of the violets shown in *Fig. 82*, and violet or a rich purple is the color best adapted for this purpose. The loops that form the petals of the violet are made over lead pencils, as shown in *Fig. 83 (a)*. Place two pencils side by side and between them place the piece of ribbon, taking care that the ends of the ribbon are of equal lengths. Wrap the upper end of the ribbon over the upper pencil and bring it up between the pencils. Wrap the lower end of the ribbon up around the lower pencil and draw it down between the pencils. There will then be one loop around each pencil, and the ribbons will be crossed in the form of an **X** between the pencils. Cut a piece of silk-covered fine wire 8 in. long, slip it up between the pencils, wrap it once around the crossed ribbons, and twist it once. Next, make a second loop around the upper pencil with the upper end of ribbon and a third loop around the lower pencil with the lower end of ribbon, as before, and at the point where they cross between the pencils, wrap the fine wire around them and twist it tightly. Repeat these operations until four loops have been made on each pencil as shown. Be very careful to keep

the satin face of the ribbon outwards, which can easily be done by giving the ribbon a half-twist each time it is passed between the pencils.

When the eight loops have been made and bound with the fine wire at the center, slip them off the pencils and crush the centers together so as to make the petals of the flowers spread out properly as in *Fig. 83 (b)*, leaving the two ends of the fine silk-covered wire hanging the length of about 3 in. Next, wrap the wires with the two ends of the ribbon, as shown in *(c)*, thus covering the stem and completing the flower. The ends of the ribbon should be knotted around the stem, to prevent them from untwisting. Make each of the remaining violets in the same manner. In *Fig. 82* nine violets are used in the cluster, but more or less may be used, should a larger or a smaller cluster be required. Pick up the violets one at a time, curve the stems slightly, arrange them together artistically, and fasten fern and violet leaves in with the flowers. A bunch of violets with a wild rose and foliage is shown in the illustration. Not only are clusters of violets used for corsage bouquets, but they are quite frequently worn on fur wraps in the middle of the winter.

Fig. 82

Fig. 83

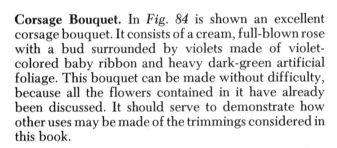

Fig. 84

Fig. 85

Corsage Bouquet. In *Fig. 84* is shown an excellent corsage bouquet. It consists of a cream, full-blown rose with a bud surrounded by violets made of violet-colored baby ribbon and heavy dark-green artificial foliage. This bouquet can be made without difficulty, because all the flowers contained in it have already been discussed. It should serve to demonstrate how other uses may be made of the trimmings considered in this book.

Petunias. The spray of petunias shown in *Fig. 85 (a)* requires ⅞ yd. of No. 16 ribbon, each flower being made of a circle of ribbon 1⅞ in. in diameter. One-half yard of No. 60 ribbon, which is twice as wide as the No. 16, might be used if two circles are cut out side by side. The petunias may be made of taffeta, satin, chiffon, or velvet. Cut a piece of paper to the shape of a perfect circle having a diameter of 1⅞ in., and with this as a pattern cut sixteen circles from the ribbon. Turn in the edge of each circle to a depth of ⅛ in. and gather it all the way around, as shown in *(b)*. Draw the thread tightly together and tie the ends. Cut a piece of fine green wire 4 in. long, double one end over, twist it, and sew the doubled end to the center of the back of the gathered circle of material, as in *(c)*. Thread an embroidery needle with heavy rope silk* of the same color, or of a contrasting color, make a knot in the thread, push the

needle through from the back, and draw the thread tightly so that the knot will be hidden in the shirrings at the back of the flower. Make a French knot in the center of the flower and then fasten the thread at the back.

Prepare each of the remaining flowers in the manner just described, and then twist the wire stems together. The flowers may be intermingled with foliage, or clustered into long sprays as shown in *Fig. 85*, or bunched so that they will have the form of a ball. They can also be appliquéd onto a foundation. If they are made of taffeta silk, without wire stems, they may be sewed on bands to be used as a trimming, also to make artistic corsage bouquets or trimmings for sash or belt. Another variation of the same arrangement is made by substituting two or three small stamens for the center instead of the French knot.

Dahlias and Sunflowers. Dahlias and sunflowers may be developed in the same manner as the petal-and-ruffle rosette shown in *Fig. 51*. In making such flowers, however, the ruffle in the center should be omitted, and instead a center should be formed by working chain-stitches with a heavy rope silk* of rich, warm brown, beginning in the center and working round and round and packing them close together. The petals should, of course, be made of the proper color of ribbon, and to make the flower appear realistic appropriate artifical foliage should be used in connection with it.

---

*Use ¹/₁₆″-wide ribbon or pearl cotton.

†Use ¹/₁₆″-wide ribbon or pearl cotton.

METRIC CONVERSION CHART

CONVERTING INCHES TO CENTIMETERS AND YARDS TO METERS

mm — millimeters   cm — centimeters   m — meters

INCHES INTO MILLIMETERS AND CENTIMETERS
(Slightly rounded off for convenience)

inches	mm		cm	inches	cm	inches	cm	inches	cm
⅛	3mm			5	12.5	21	53.5	38	96.5
¼	6mm			5½	14	22	56	39	99
⅜	10mm	or	1cm	6	15	23	58.5	40	101.5
½	13mm	or	1.3cm	7	18	24	61	41	104
⅝	15mm	or	1.5cm	8	20.5	25	63.5	42	106.5
¾	20mm	or	2cm	9	23	26	66	43	109
⅞	22mm	or	2.2cm	10	25.5	27	68.5	44	112
1	25mm	or	2.5cm	11	28	28	71	45	114.5
1¼	32mm	or	3.2cm	12	30.5	29	73.5	46	117
1½	38mm	or	3.8cm	13	33	30	76	47	119.5
1¾	45mm	or	4.5cm	14	35.5	31	79	48	122
2	50mm	or	5cm	15	38	32	81.5	49	124.5
2½	65mm	or	6.5cm	16	40.5	33	84	50	127
3	75mm	or	7.5cm	17	43	34	86.5		
3½	90mm	or	9cm	18	46	35	89		
4	100mm	or	10cm	19	48.5	36	91.5		
4½	115mm	or	11.5cm	20	51	37	94		

YARDS TO METERS
(Slightly rounded off for convenience)

yards	meters	yards	meters	yards	meters	yards	meters	yards	meters
⅛	0.15	2⅛	1.95	4⅛	3.80	6⅛	5.60	8⅛	7.45
¼	0.25	2¼	2.10	4¼	3.90	6¼	5.75	8¼	7.55
⅜	0.35	2⅜	2.20	4⅜	4.00	6⅜	5.85	8⅜	7.70
½	0.50	2½	2.30	4½	4.15	6½	5.95	8½	7.80
⅝	0.60	2⅝	2.40	4⅝	4.25	6⅝	6.10	8⅝	7.90
¾	0.70	2¾	2.55	4¾	4.35	6¾	6.20	8¾	8.00
⅞	0.80	2⅞	2.65	4⅞	4.50	6⅞	6.30	8⅞	8.15
1	0.95	3	2.75	5	4.60	7	6.40	9	8.25
1⅛	1.05	3⅛	2.90	5⅛	4.70	7⅛	6.55	9⅛	8.35
1¼	1.15	3¼	3.00	5¼	4.80	7¼	6.65	9¼	8.50
1⅜	1.30	3⅜	3.10	5⅜	4.95	7⅜	6.75	9⅜	8.60
1½	1.40	3½	3.20	5½	5.05	7½	6.90	9½	8.70
1⅝	1.50	3⅝	3.35	5⅝	5.15	7⅝	7.00	9⅝	8.80
1¾	1.60	3¾	3.45	5¾	5.30	7¾	7.10	9¾	8.95
1⅞	1.75	3⅞	3.55	5⅞	5.40	7⅞	7.20	9⅞	9.05
2	1.85	4	3.70	6	5.50	8	7.35	10	9.15